This Book Belongs to :

Copyright ©2023
By Contigo Wellness

All rights reserved.

No portion of this book may be reproduced
in any form without written permission
from the publisher or author,
except as permitted by U.S. copyright law.

TÚ IMPORTAS

YOU MATTER

SOY FUERTE Y HERMOSA

MENTAL HEALTH IS WEALTH

IT'S OKAY TO NOT BE OKAY

SELF-CARE IS A PRIORITY

HOY NO ES EL FIN DE LA HISTORIA

LA MENTE ES PODEROSA; ALIMÉNTALA BIEN

EVERY DAY IS AN OPPORTUNITY TO HEAL

TÚ ERES SUFICIENTE

YOU ARE STRONGER THAN YOU THINK

SELF-CARE IS NOT SELFISH

THE MIND IS A GARDEN; TEND TO IT

IT'S OKAY TO TALK TO SOMEONE

MENTAL HEALTH MATTERS

TU SALUD MENTAL ES VALIOSA

SOY UNA GUERRERA PODEROSA

EVERY STEP IS AN ACHIEVEMENT

NO ESTÁS SOLO EN ESTO

SELF-LOVE IS ESSENTIAL

ESTOY EN EQUILIBRIO CON LA VIDA

I PROMOTE PEACE AND HARMONY

TÚ PUEDES SUPERARLO

TU BIENESTAR ES IMPORTANTE

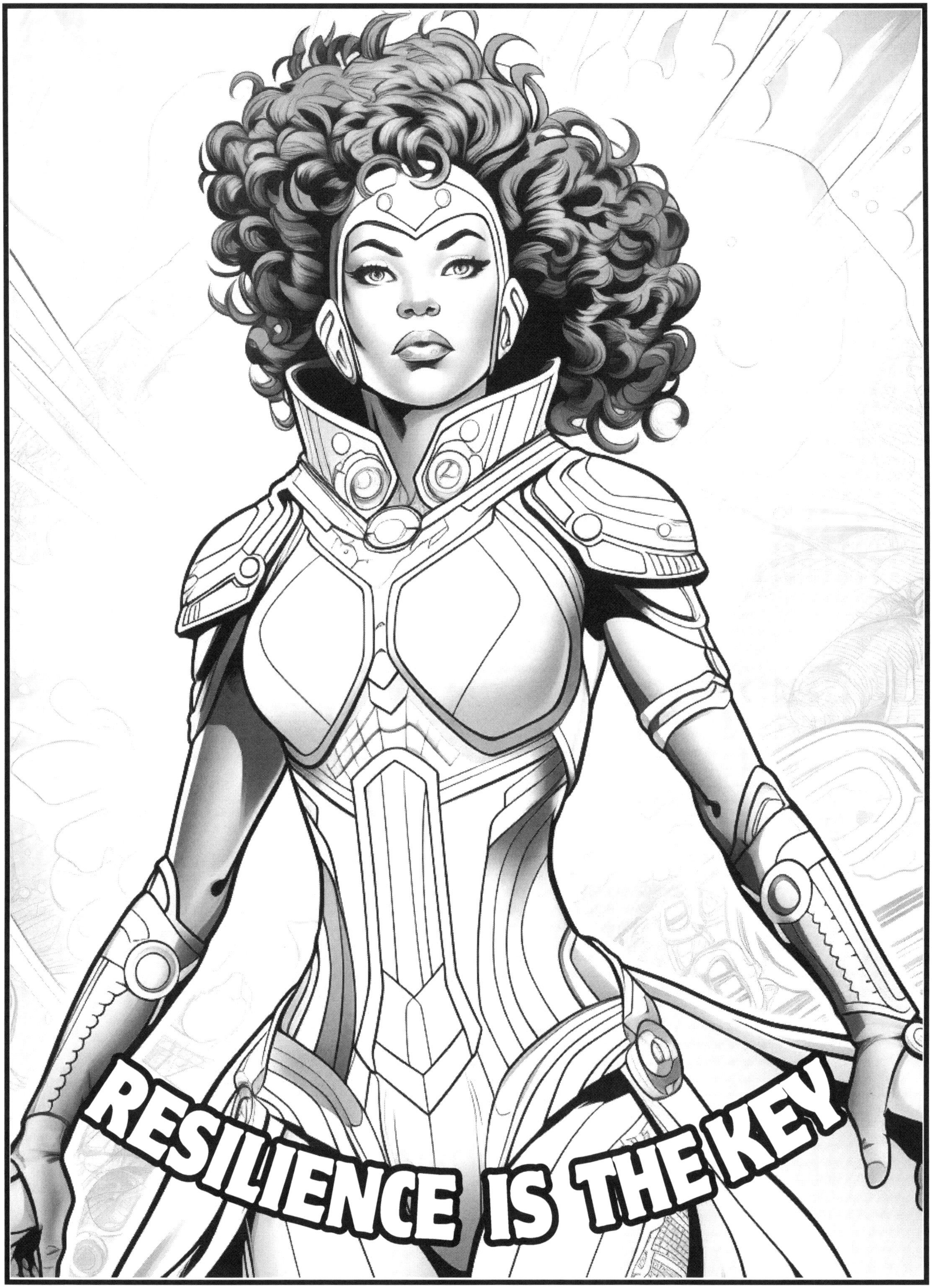
RESILIENCE IS THE KEY

STRENGTH COMES FROM WITHIN

MI CORAZÓN ES FUERTE

SOY UNA LUCHADORA

Made in the USA
Columbia, SC
06 August 2024